Insomnia's Ink

a poetry collection

Susie Clevenger

This is a work of fiction. Names, characters, places, and incidents either are the product of the author's imagination or are used fictitiously. Any resemblance to actual persons, living or dead, events, or locales is entirely coincidental.

Wings O'Butterfly Publishing

Cover design by Scott Morgan

Table of Contents

This is dedicated to all the insomniacs who pace
the bridge between night and day.

Introduction

My poetry seems to prefer the late shift, the tick of a clock, the moon peeking through the windows. Much of what I write is born from insomnia; those long hours that rattle my brain with emotions daylight can't handle. *Insomnia's Ink* is a glimpse into thoughts that keep me up at night.

Midnight

Graveyard Shift

A small lamp illuminates
a dog-eared journal
where cluttered words
spill in bits and phrases
from insomnia's pen.....

Poetry works the graveyard shift.

Currency of Dreams

I stow words deep in my pockets
along with sea shells, stones,
and bits of glass.

They are treasures, currency of dreams.
When I can't speak, they are my voice.
When I can't walk, they are my journey.

My voice fragile as a faded alphabet
separates meaning from silence.
Ink weeps discovery across an empty page.

Heavy Hand

Sunset honey spoons the horizon
with summer memories in those
tiny moments before ebony snatches smiles.

I watch the keeper of secrets unfold her cloak
in the breath between comfort and haunting.

Your hand is heavy, Night, upon my brow.
I haven't a knife to cut light into the fingerprints
you leave upon my dreams.

I have no animosity for the moon or stars.
They sing of forgetting, but your murky palm
pushes me deeper into a river of pain.

Scissor me from this play of fright that steals rest.
Night, I beg….Please come without a burden.
Your heavy hand weights my peace.

Three Days of Breath

Star eyes see tomorrow
through threads spun
into length of days.

A question rocks
three days of breath
before what will be is sealed.

Fed from the moon's breast
infant dreams spill from cradle
to first dust of dawn.

With thread and knife fate
arrives to cut life into hours
that can never be changed.

Blood House

In this blood house of my genetics
where ancestry has determined skin and bone
I wonder if this knifed clay bears a deeper
resemblance
to spirit than my face reanimating death.

Are the words that come when sleep evades
the poems of another's dreams released
on a sea of stars to reach the sand of my pen?

Names hang on a family tree where mirrors see
but can't hear...Somewhere in the puzzle I am a
verse.

Trapped Rhyme

Night writes another verse
across my temples.
I feel the throbbing ink
of so many yesterdays
bleeding down my cheeks.

My heart keeps beating
in its normal rhythm
oblivious to the rhyme
trapped between my teeth.

Fence

Gossip has a choir
eager for a new song
and scratches at my
throat to find the melody.

You pry, demand,
attempt to peel layers
from secrets etched on
my ribcage…

Trust is a coin earned in
the belly of intuition.

It's evident you'll never
earn a wage behind razor wire
marked *No Trespassing*.

Separating Seeds From Intent

We sit at the same table
separating seeds from intent.
Our chosen stances grip the X
until eye to eye kills compromise.
We have become a field where
nothing grows except division.

Your Burden

You strapped secrets to my bones
and needled my tongue until
a promise to never tell pooled on my lips.

While you dance around the sun
I walk the dark side of the moon
storing silence between stones.

I mourn the voice I sacrificed to faith
your errors would rebirth change.
Alone strangles me with your burden.

Kool-Aid and Brimstone

We drank the Kool-Aid
and searched the horizon
for the end of the world.

With our boots laced to brimstone
we toured damnation until
love was supplanted by fear.

Summer stirs my unholy ghosts
with their songs of blood echoing
through the questions I never asked.

I still feel the pain of wearing wool.

Change of Heart

They want to glue me to their view;
paste me as cooperative so there
won't be any discord from different.

My eyes once held the glint of absolutes.
I recognize the self-righteous stare and
voices echoing in scriptured tongues.

Life has cut the artery of my judgment
and I bleed grief from my spirit
at the depths of my rejection.

I can't choose another's path so I won't
surrender my shoes to the footfalls of another.
The greatest commandment is to love.

I struggle…I'm incomplete…I am learning.

Sing Away My Scars

Nightingale, this night is too dark
without your song to rock me to sleep.
Lonely has wrapped me in its scars
and I can't feel love any more.

Who is this songstress of melancholy
that begs my throat to sing
a melody to devour pain?

I cling to this limb scented with spring
and only wish to commune with the moon,
but her tears can't go unanswered.

Dear one, absence nurses its wounds
only as long as you allow...
Be the light for another until
you've burnt the darkness from alone.

I will sing for you until your dreams
carry you to truth...Until you trust
you can fly without my wings.

An Open Wound

Poetry is a window into secrets,
ink confessions of a strange mind
that refuses to sleep on an open wound.

Suspended between truth and lie,
night and day, beginning and end,
I take shallow breaths of incomplete.

Watching sunrise melt stars on the horizon
I wonder if noon will find me still sorting
through words whispering in my head.

Birdsong

Moon Fed On Imagination

Gravel dust feathered the nest
of our four rooms and five souls
in three acres of show me state.

Born middle child loud
I was a dandelion extrovert
in a garden of solitary.

Moon fed on imagination
through screen wire I tucked words
into hours until dreams found ink.

Under school house lamplight
where a raven spoke in Poe's voice
I found poetry could make sense of my noise.

Birth on Canvas

The canvas, open thighed
with birthing pains begs
my brush to be its midwife.

Inadequate but inspired
I deliver the newborn
with strokes of paint
across pallor's cheek.

Rooted in burnt umber,
a trunk sprouts leaves of gold
and peach nippled fruit.

When my muse speaks
it is finished, I feel relief,
but in this brief respite
I hear the first moans
calling from another womb.

Pickled Thoughts Without Fins

I ice skate
on a salt mirror
chasing clouds

while drops
of blue sky splash
my ankles with summer.

Lost in the mirage
of pickled thoughts
without fins I skim

the briney surface wishing
I could dive into the glass refection
to swim through the yellow sun.

Sticky Notes or Dreams

Chance has no history
to learn from, or prayers
to answer. It can't predict
the who and when of favor.

It's the thin air of possibility
where we attach sticky notes
hoping fate can read
our handwriting.

Dreams on the other hand
require sturdy boots
and resolve to trek the
stony ground of question marks.

I Will Dance On Your Silence

Pour salt in my wounds
and I will best you by healing.

My life is too short to carry
a gallon of tears on my chest.

If you swallow your tongue
from the bloat of your words,
I will dance on your silence.

I am no longer petals begging for light,
but a blossomed flower in full sun.

Years Float From Scissors

I no longer carry you
in my hair.

Years float
from scissors
to the floor
and I am free.

The hate you sprinkled
in my starlight now
mixes with dirt.

A broom waits to
remove the last tie to your
midnight voice.

My eyes are brighter,
bluer, wider, at peace.

I no longer carry you
in my hair.

The Song of a Rose

She blossoms in the
tile echo of midnight
and the needle drip
of medicine seeking
a vein to riddle.

When the valley seems too long
her voice steals the breath from doubt
to fill the air with the music of healing.

A beautiful porcelain skin rose
she transcends the concrete garden
where why never finds an answer
and sings a new song of morning.

Pictures of the Silver Lining

A beautiful face,
a theater of eyes
and smiles, captures
my heart with
its animation.

When anxious days
cloud with shrouds
of dismay, I dance
among images of light
pressed between
glass and frame.

She is my child, a gift
filled with bursts of laughter,
a tigress with comedic timing,
arms that hug away the hell
riffling through my spirit.

A beautiful face, a theater of eyes
and smiles, erasing pain until
I can feel the silver lining.

Sandpaper Stars

Sandpaper stars know
best is brighter than
the last surrender into
blemished expectations.

Callous words can not
steal light life has earned
from a baptism of fire.

Time lapsed rapture
left us sipping nicotine
from gamma rays where
we were fashioned in
a cloud of dust.

We hang tattered, but whole
in a sapphire universe,
forgiving, forgetting,
overcoming the sanded speech
that tried to strip away our radiance.

The Cult of Dreaming Thesaurus

They dance naked in metaphors
speaking this – meaning that,
winding words into introspection.

Heads bent over a thesaurus prayer book
word artisans seek the holy grail of vocabulary
to eradicate the perception of recycled thought.

Under a lightbulb sky poets seek the blessing
of Bragi as poetry travels from mind to print
in a soul spill of imagery and imagination.

Dear Poets...My Poets

I am drawn to your words
like a moth devouring light.
When the world tears another
layer from shell I inhabit,
your words fill the scar and speak
another day into my flesh.

Dear poets...my poets...
Yes, I claim you as my own.
You speak the unspeakable,
take my pain, and leave me whole.

Better View

Crushed flower petals
bear the scent or nirvana,
but the other side of the fence
is a stair climb to open air
so blind eyes can have
a better view of heaven.

Feather Throat

Mired in self and day old dread
I sat in the wind song of a mockingbird
greeting dawn and felt my spirit
reach to touch the feather throat of joy.

Connected to light the darkness I had hoarded
lifted its tentacles from my tongue to allow
the blessed words of I Am to have expression.

Acknowledgements

Dawn, you are my porcelain rose.

Carrie, you are the laughter in the silver lining.

Charlie, you are the keeper of my heart.

About the Author

Susie Clevenger is an author, poet, and amateur photographer. She was first published at the age of fifteen in *Missouri Youth Write*. She is author of the poetry collection, *Dirt Road Dreams*. Her work has been featured in the online publications, *The Creative Nexus, Poetry & Prose Magazine, The Brinks Gallery, The Global Twitter Community Poetry Project*, and *Journey of the Heart*. She is a member of the Academy of American Poets, The Poetry Society of Texas and coordinator for the Blog Talk Radio program the Creative Nexus Café™. Susie resides in Houston, Texas with her husband, Charlie.

Where to find Susie:

www.susieclevenger.com

Like on Facebook.com:
www.facebook.com/susieclevengerpoetry

Her blog:
www.confessionsofalaundrygoddess.blogspot.com

Follow on Twitter.com @wingsobutterfly

Blog Talk Radio ~ Creative Nexus Café™
http://www.blogtalkradio.com/creativenexus

Amazon.com Author Page:
http://www.amazon.com/Susie-
Clevenger/e/B00AQNQWTO

www.ingramcontent.com/pod-product-compliance
Lightning Source LLC
Chambersburg PA
CBHW030305030426
42337CB00012B/596